Hans-Günter Heumann

Dreamworld

20 Easy Romantic Piano Pieces
20 leichte romantische Klavierstücke
20 pièces romantiques faciles pour piano

ED 23709
ISMN 979-0-001-21794-1
ISBN 978-3-7957-3088-8

www.schott-music.com

Mainz · London · Madrid · Paris · New York · Tokyo · Beijing
© 2023 Schott Music GmbH & Co. KG, Mainz · Printed in Germany

Imprint / Impressum
ED 23709
ISMN 979-0-001-21794-1
ISBN 978-3-7957-3088-8
Cover: grandfailure/www.stock.adobe.com
© 2023 Schott Music GmbH & Co. KG, Mainz
Printed in Germany · BSS 60 307

Preface

Dreamworld contains 20 easy modern, romantic piano pieces from the genres of romantic pop and neoclassicism, which take the player into a dream world. Easy, varied and popular accompaniments are reminiscent of current soundtracks. All compositions have one thing in common: They are fun to play, provide relaxation, are easy to remember, and go down well with the listeners. The imaginative titles such as *Amélie in Dreamland*, *In Seventh Heaven*, *Rainbow Way*, *Every Cloud a Dream* have been turned into music in a way that stimulates the visual imagination.

This is ideal, varied and fascinating supplementary material for every advanced beginner, which can be mastered quickly and is well suited for lessons, for playing in one's free time and for first auditions.

The pieces are in easy keys containing no more than one accidental. Everything has been edited for educational purposes and provided with tempo indications, fingerings and dynamics. Recordings are available on leading streaming portals such as Apple Music, Spotify or YouTube.

I hope you enjoy these pieces.
Hans-Günter Heumann

Vorwort

Dreamworld enthält 20 leichte, moderne, romantische Klavierstücke aus den Genres Romantic Pop und Neoklassik, die den Spieler/die Spielerin in eine Traumwelt entführen. Einfache, abwechslungsreiche und beliebte Begleitfiguren erinnern an aktuelle Filmmusik. Alle Kompositionen haben eines gemeinsam: Sie machen einfach Spaß, bieten Entspannung, sind einprägsam und kommen bei Zuhörenden gut an. Die fantasievollen Titel wie *Amélie im Traumland*, *Im siebten Himmel*, *Regenbogen-Weg*, *Jede Wolke ein Traum* sind musikalisch so umgesetzt worden, dass die bildliche Vorstellungskraft angeregt wird.

Ein ideales, abwechslungsreiches und faszinierendes Ergänzungsmaterial für jeden fortgeschrittenen Anfänger, das schnell zu erlernen ist und sich gut für Unterricht, Freizeit und erste Vorspiele eignet.

Die Spielstücke stehen in einfachen Tonarten mit bis zu einem Vorzeichen. Alles ist pädagogisch aufbereitet und mit Tempoangaben, Fingersätzen und Dynamik versehen. Aufnahmen sind auf führenden Streaming-Portalen wie Apple Music, Spotify oder YouTube abrufbar.

Viel Freude mit den Stücken wünscht
Hans-Günter Heumann

Préface

Dreamworld contient 20 morceaux de piano faciles, modernes et romantiques, issus des genres pop romantique et néo-classique, qui transportent le joueur/la joueuse dans un monde imaginaire. Des figures d'accompagnement faciles, variées et populaires font penser aux musiques de film actuelles. Toutes les compositions ont un point commun : Elles sont plaisantes à jouer, permettent de se détendre, sont faciles à retenir et sont bien accueillies par les auditeurs. Les titres imaginatifs comme *Amélie au pays des rêves*, *Au septième ciel*, *Chemin de l'arc-en-ciel*, *Chaque nuage un rêve* ont été transformés en musique de manière à stimuler l'imagination visuelle.

Il s'agit d'un matériel complémentaire idéal, varié et fascinant pour tout débutant avancé, qui peut être maîtrisé rapidement et qui se prête bien à des cours, des loisirs et des premières auditions.

Les morceaux sont dans des tonalités faciles n'ayant pas plus d'une altération. Tout est préparé de manière pédagogique et contient des indications de tempo, de doigté et de dynamique. Les enregistrements sont disponibles sur les principaux portails de streaming comme Apple Music, Spotify ou YouTube.

Je vous souhaite beaucoup de plaisir avec ces morceaux.
Hans-Günter Heumann

Contents / Inhalt / Contenu

Amélie in Dreamland

Amélie im Traumland / Amélie au pays des rêves

Hans-Günter Heumann
(*1955)

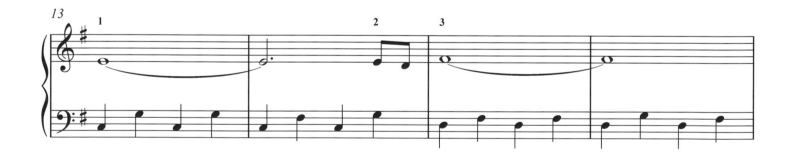

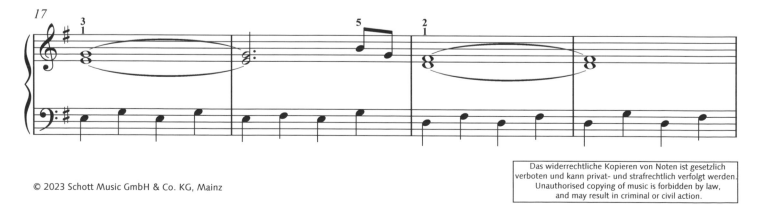

Moonlit Night

Mondnacht / Nuit de lune

Hans-Günter Heumann

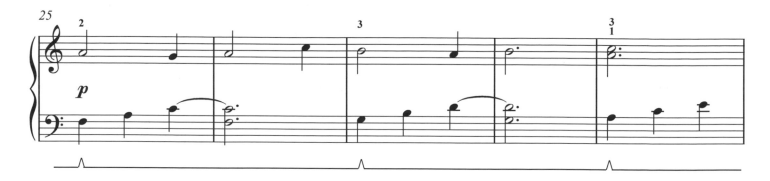

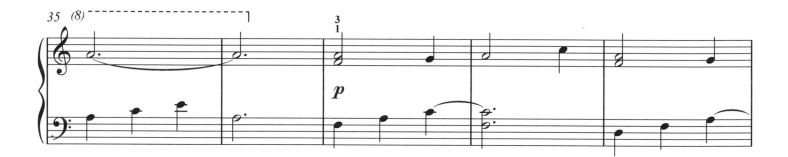

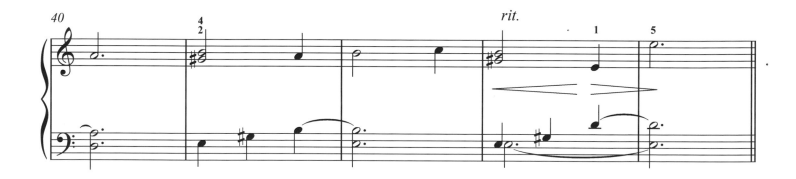

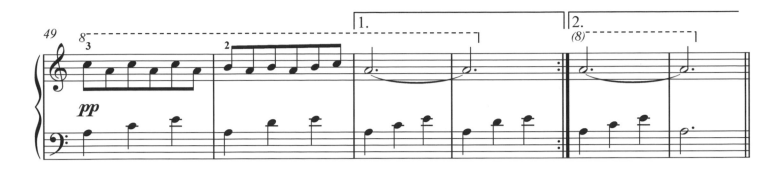

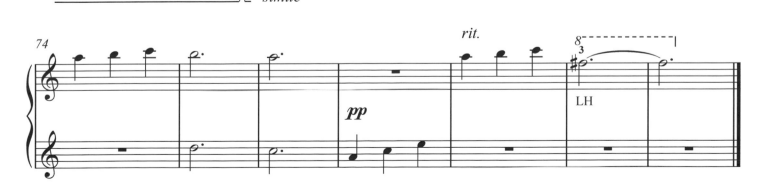

In Seventh Heaven

Im siebten Himmel / Au septième ciel

Hans-Günter Heumann

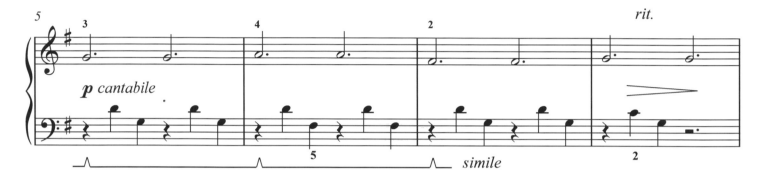

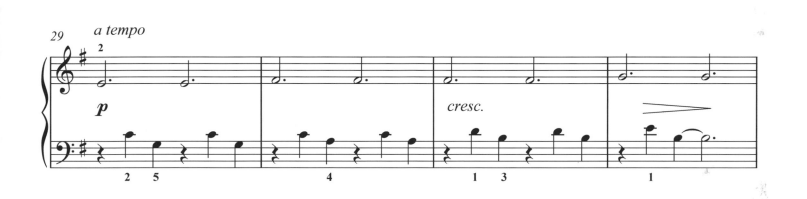

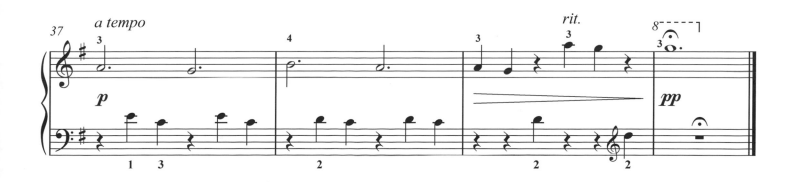

Reverie at the Piano

Träumerei am Klavier / Rêverie au piano

Hans-Günter Heumann

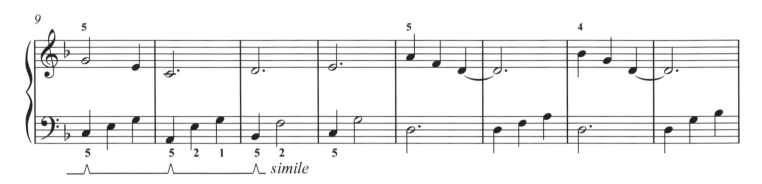

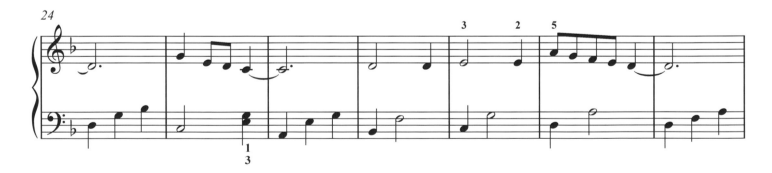

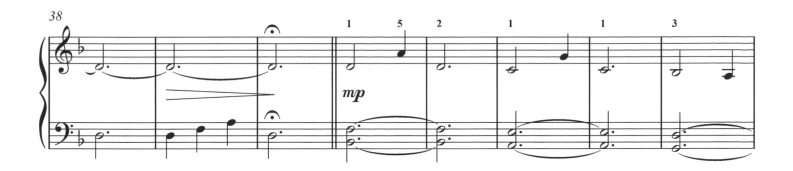

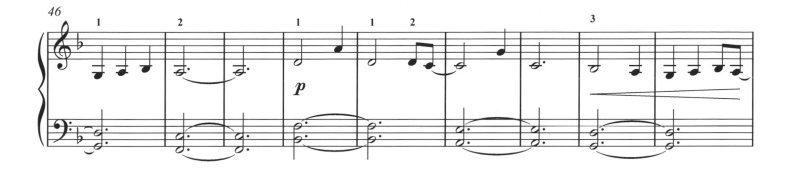

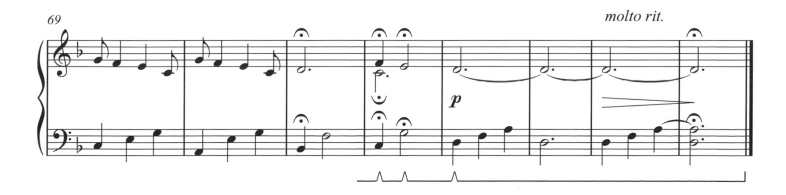

Sunset
Sonnenuntergang / Coucher du soleil

Hans-Günter Heumann

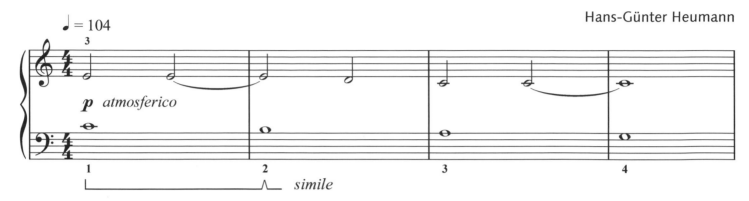

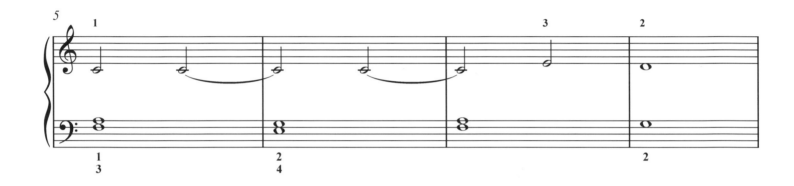

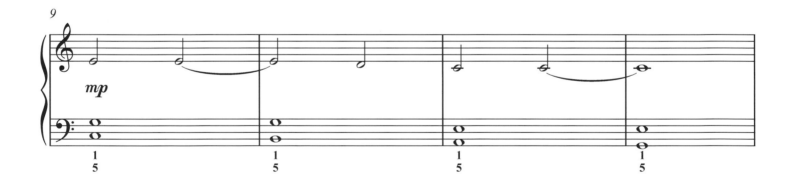

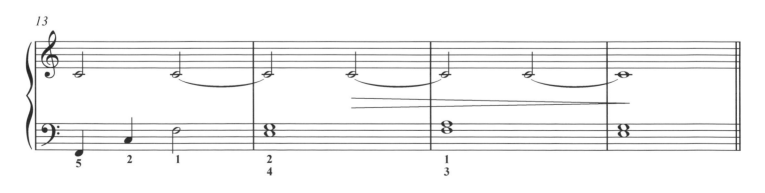

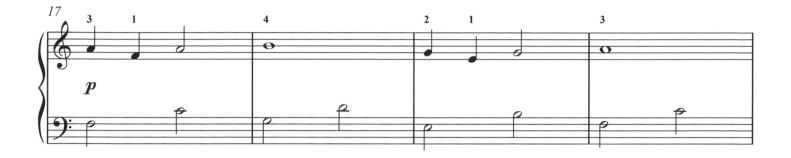

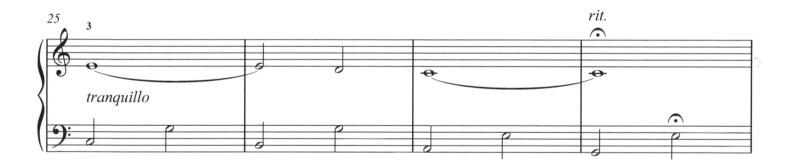

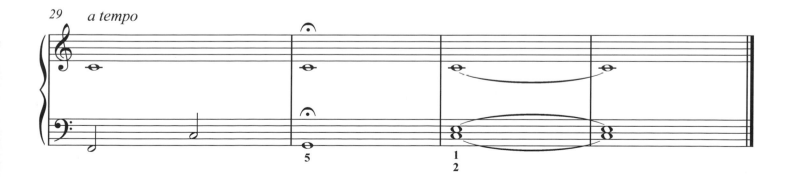

Moments of Love
Momente der Liebe / Moments d'amour

Hans-Günter Heumann

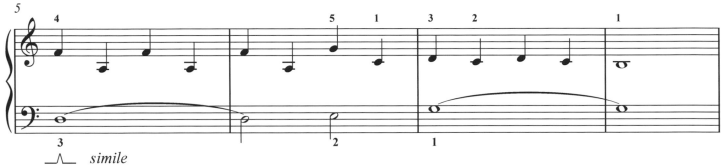

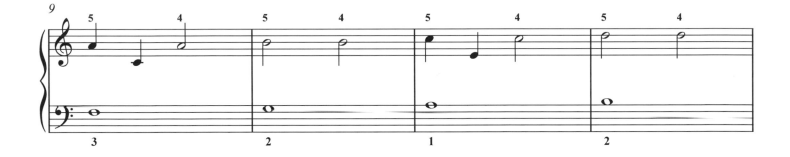

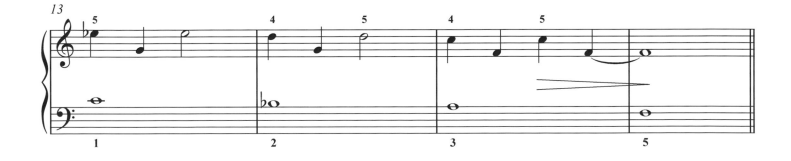

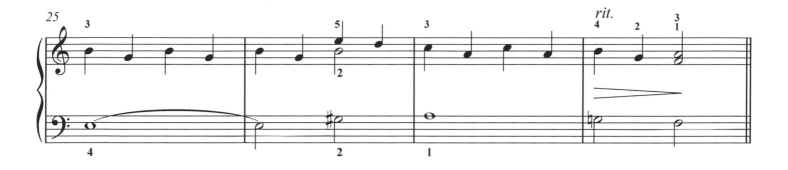

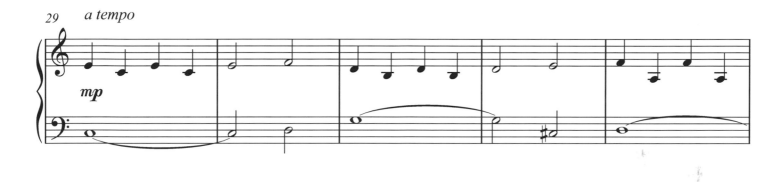

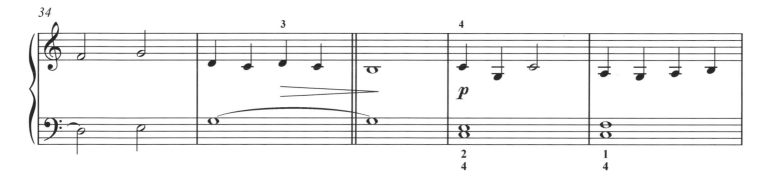

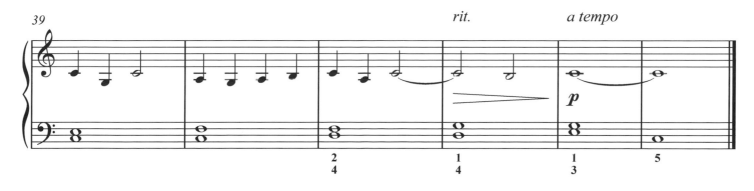

Rainbow Path

Regenbogenweg / Chemin de l'arc-en-ciel

Hans-Günter Heumann

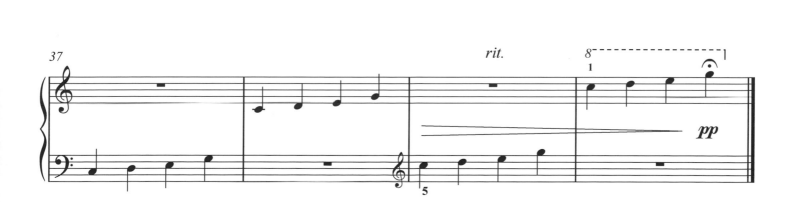

Realm of Sounds
Reich der Klänge / Royaume des sons

Hans-Günter Heumann

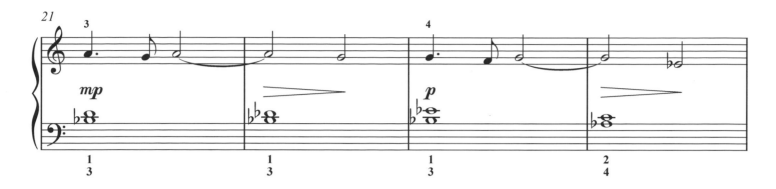

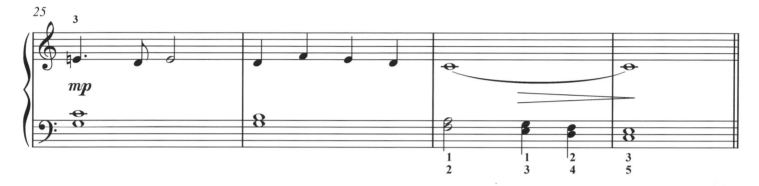

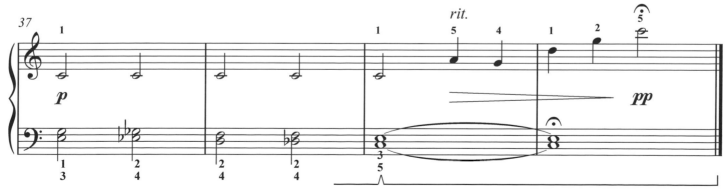

Soul Painting
Seelenmalerei / Peinture de l'âme

Hans-Günter Heumann

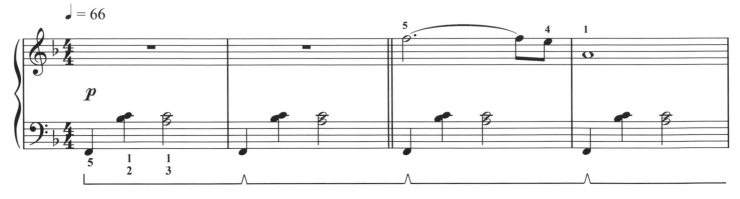

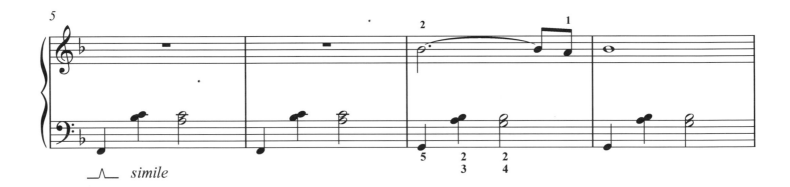

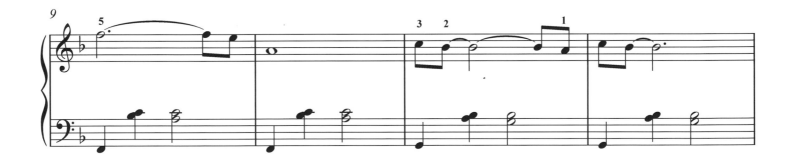

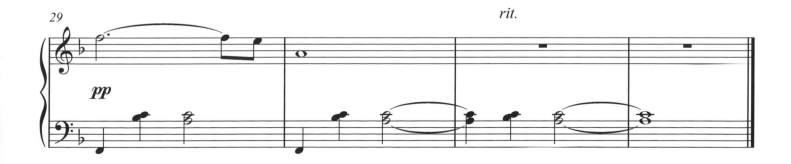

Light and Shadow
Licht und Schatten / Lumière et ombre

Hans-Günter Heumann

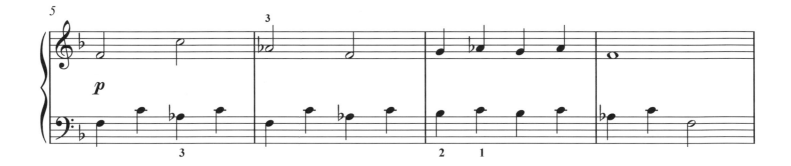

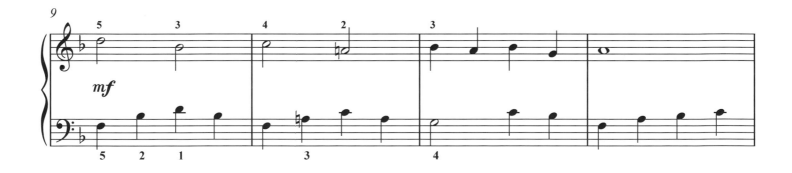

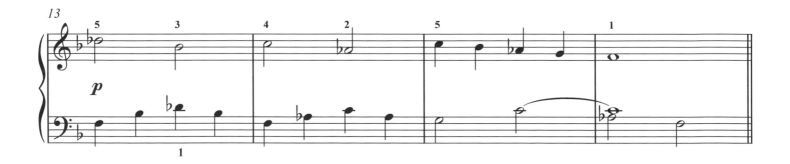

Polar Lights
Polarlichter / Aurores polaires

Hans-Günter Heumann

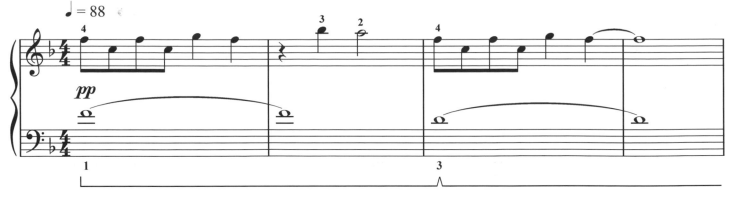

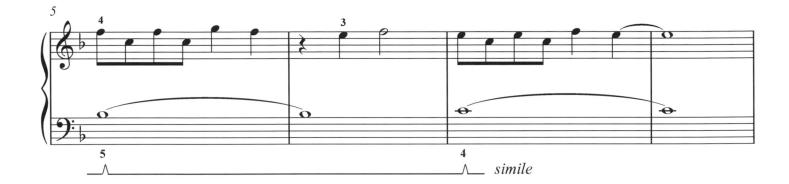

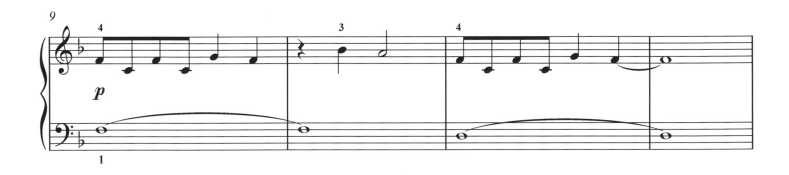

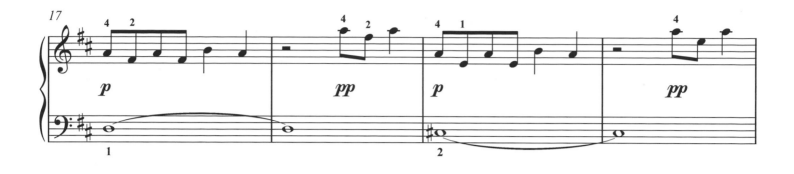

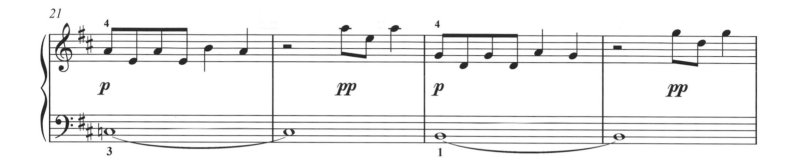

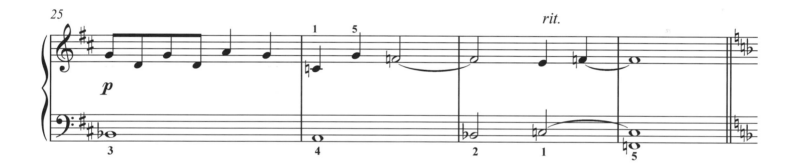

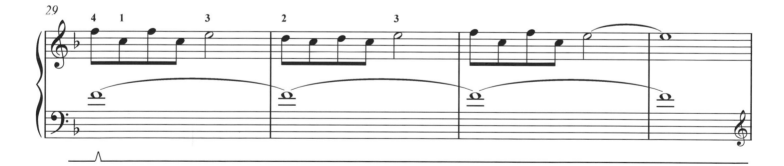

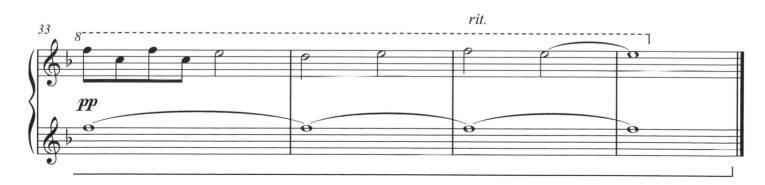

The Magic of Beginnings
Der Zauber des Anfangs / La magie du début

Hans-Günter Heumann

32

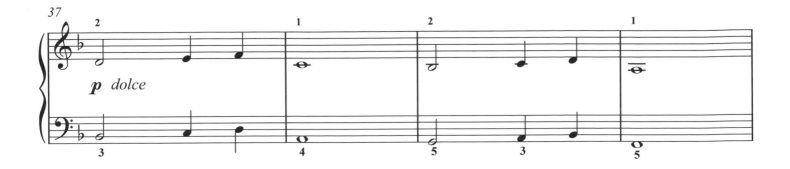

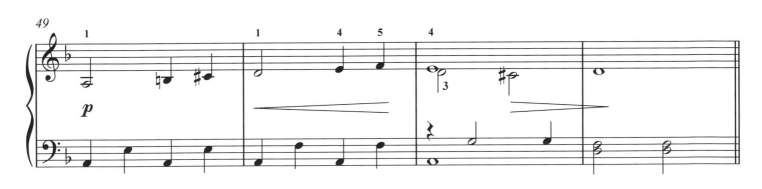

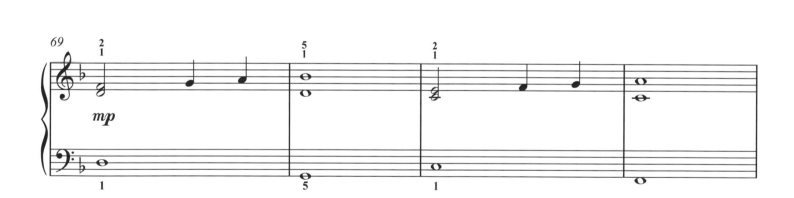

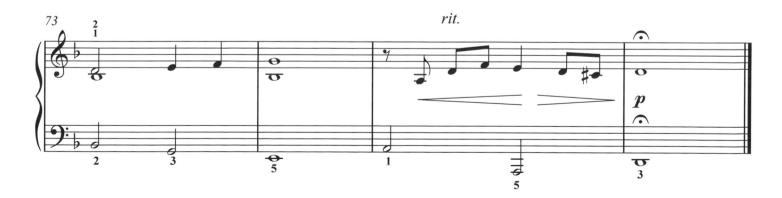

Let Your Heart Speak

Lass dein Herz sprechen / Laisse parler ton cœur

Hans-Günter Heumann

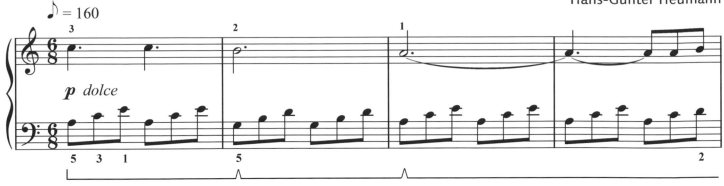

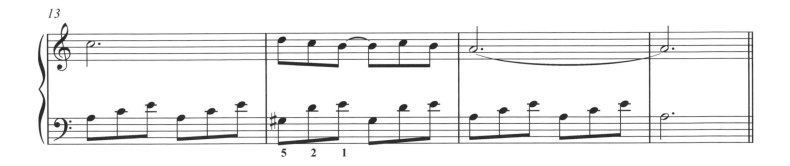

The Hidden Paradise

Das versteckte Paradies / Le paradis caché

Hans-Günter Heumann

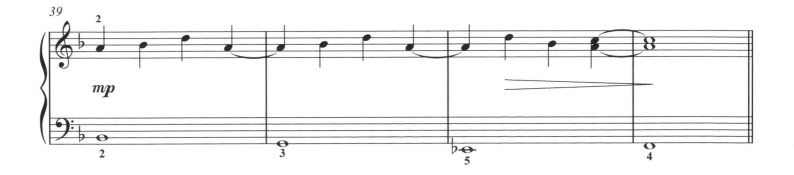

Freely

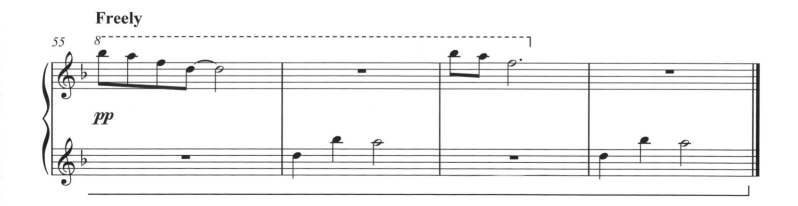

Every Cloud a Dream

Jede Wolke ein Traum / Chaque nuage un rêve

Hans-Günter Heumann

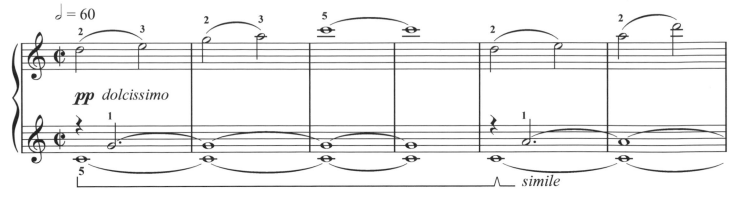

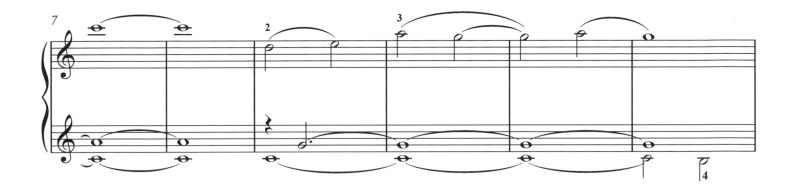

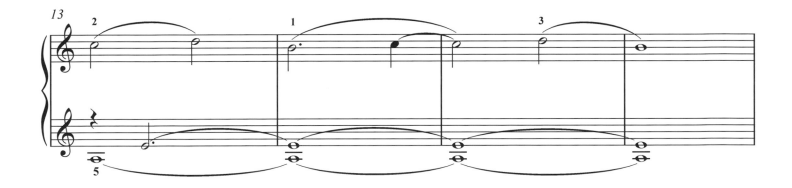

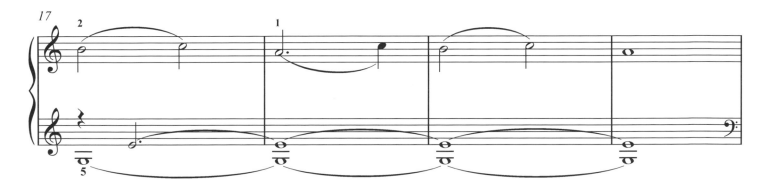

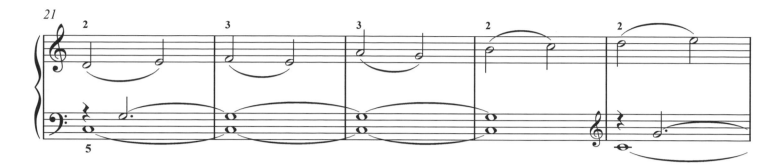

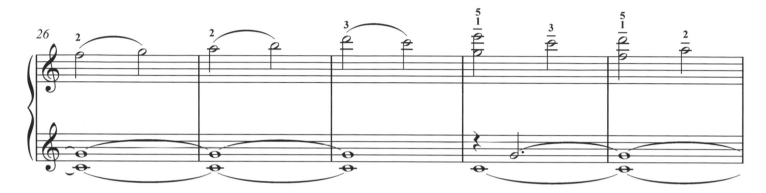

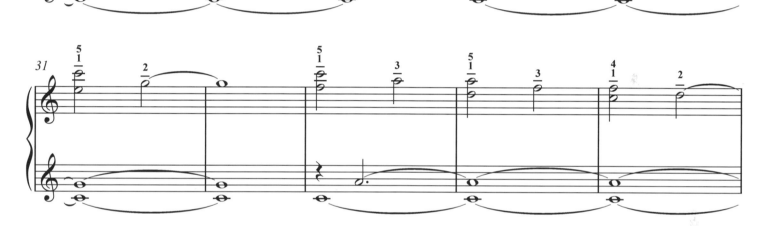

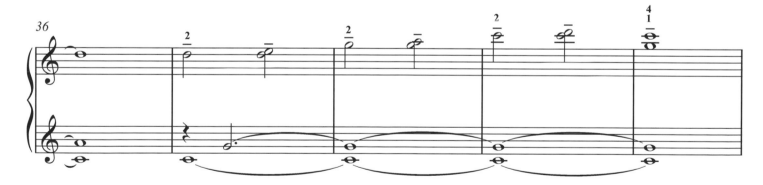

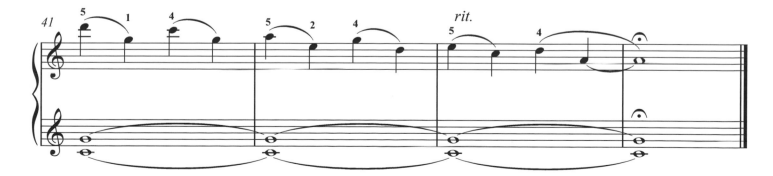

Water Lily Pond
Seerosenteich / Bassin aux nénuphars

Hans-Günter Heumann

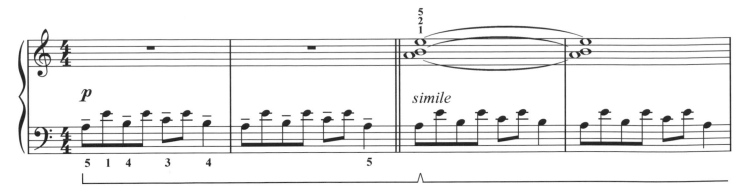

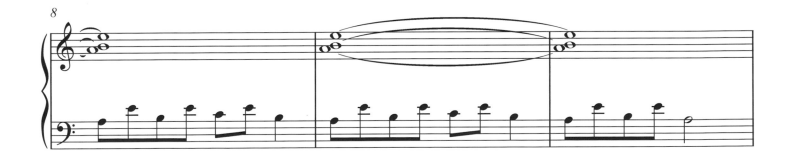

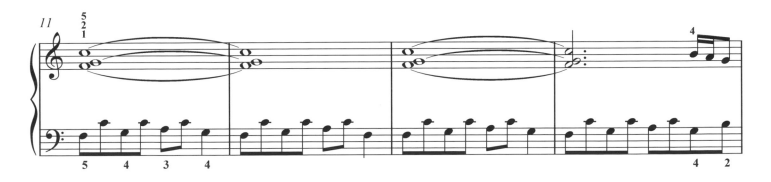

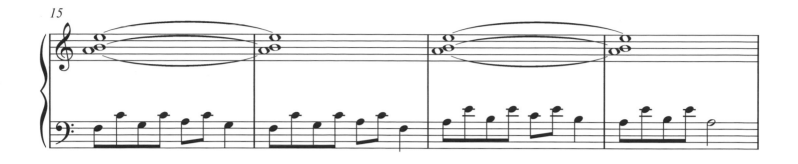

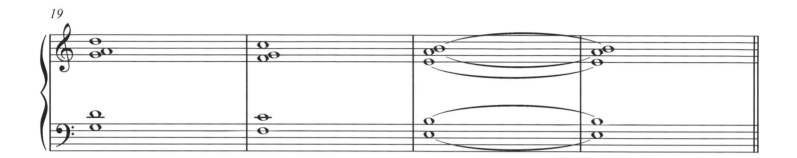

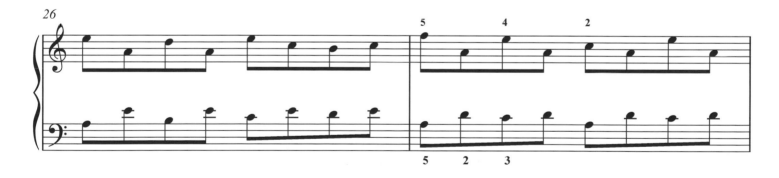

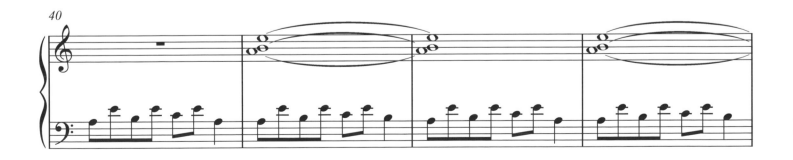

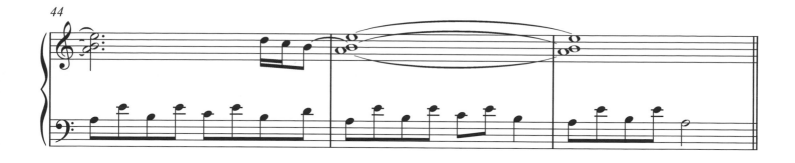

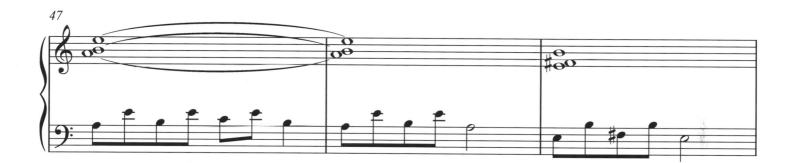

rit.   *a tempo*

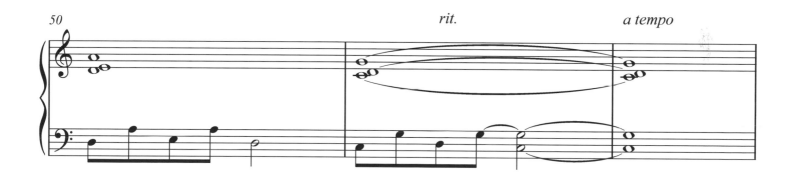

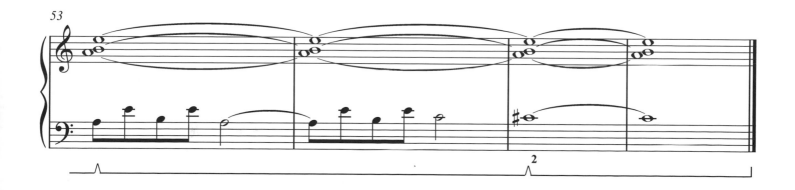

Kissed by Heaven
Von Himmel geküsst / Embrassé par le ciel

Hans-Günter Heumann

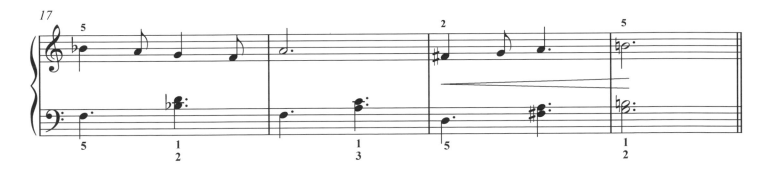

Heart's Desires

Herzenswünsche / Désirs du cœur

Hans-Günter Heumann

Rhythm of the Waves

Rhythmus der Wellen / Rythme des vagues

Hans-Günter Heumann

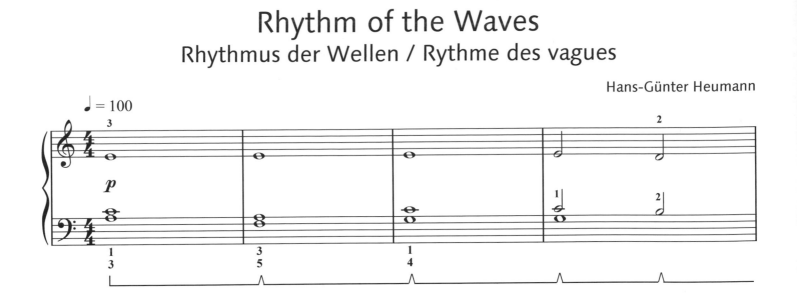

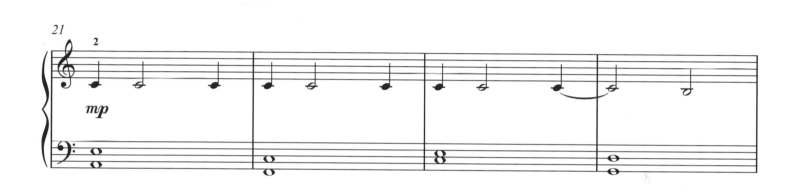

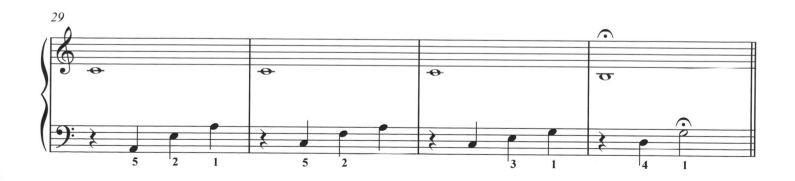

Make a Wish

Wünsch dir was / Fais un vœu

Hans-Günter Heumann

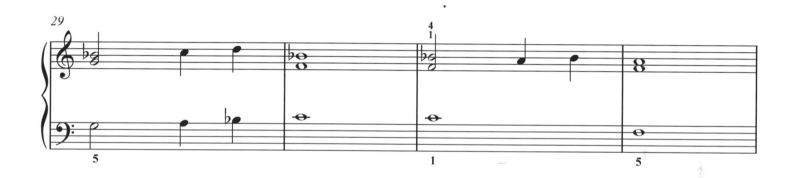

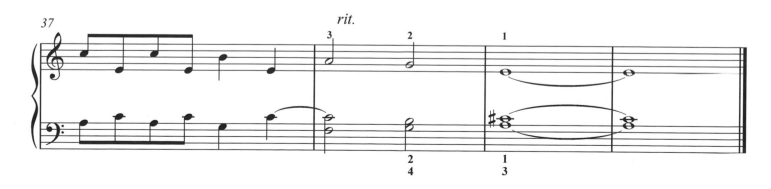

Schott Music, Mainz 60 307